Cram101 Textbook Outlines to accompany:

Operations Management

David Barnes, 1st Edition

A Content Technologies Inc. publication (c) 2011.

cram101.com

Learning System

Cram101 Textbook Outlines is a learning system. The notes in this book are the highlights of your textbook, you will never have to highlight a book again.

How to use this book. Take this book to class, it is your notebook for the lecture. The notes and highlights on the left hand side of the pages follow the outline and order of the textbook. All you have to do is follow along while your instructor presents the lecture. Circle the items emphasized in class and add other important information on the right side. With Cram101 Textbook Outlines you'll spend less time writing and more time listening. Learning becomes more efficient.

Cram101.com Online

Increase your studying efficiency by using Cram101.com's practice tests and online reference material. It is the perfect complement to Cram101 Textbook Outlines. Use self-teaching matching tests or simulate in-class testing with comprehensive multiple choice tests, or simply use Cram's true and false tests for quick review. Cram101.com even allows you to enter your in-class notes for an integrated studying format combining the textbook notes with your class notes.

Visit **www.Cram101.com**, click Sign Up at the top of the screen, and enter **DK73DW11297** in the promo code box on the registration screen. Your access to www.Cram101.com is discounted by 50% because you have purchased this book. Sign up and stop highlighting textbooks forever.

Operations Management
David Barnes, 1st

CONTENTS

Chapter 1. Operations managment

Export	The term Export is derived from the conceptual meaning as to ship the goods and services out of the port of a country. The seller of such goods and services is referred to as an `Exporter` who is based in the country of Export whereas the overseas based buyer is referred to as an `importer`. In International Trade, `Exports` refers to selling goods and services produced in home country to other markets.
G-code	G-code are functions in the Numerical control programming language. The G-codes are the codes that position the tool and do the actual work, as opposed to M-codes, that manages the machine, T for tool-related codes. S and F are tool-Speed and tool-Feed, and finally D-codes for tool compensation.
Operations management	Operations management is an area of business concerned with the production of goods and services, and involves the responsibility of ensuring that business operations are efficient in terms of using as little resource as needed, and effective in terms of meeting customer requirements. It is concerned with managing the process that converts inputs (in the forms of materials, labor and energy) into outputs (in the form of goods and services). Operations traditionally refers to the production of goods and services separately, although the distinction between these two main types of operations is increasingly difficult to make as manufacturers tend to merge product and service offerings.
Resource	A Resource is any physical or virtual entity of limited availability that needs to be consumed to obtain a benefit from it. In most cases, commercial or even ethic factors require Resource allocation through Resource management.
Customer	A Customer is usually used to refer to a current or potential buyer or user of the products of an individual or organization, called the supplier, seller, or vendor. This is typically through purchasing or renting goods or services. However, in certain contexts, the term Customer also includes by extension any entity that uses or experiences the services of another.
Information processing	Information processing is the change (processing) of information in any manner detectable by an observer. As such, it is a process which describes everything which happens (changes) in the universe, from the falling of a rock to the printing of a text file from a digital computer system. In the latter case, an information processor is changing the form of presentation of that text file.

Chapter 1. Operations managment

Back office	A Back office is a part of most corporations where tasks dedicated to running the company itself take place. The term comes from the building layout of early companies where the front office would contain the sales and other customer-facing staff and the Back office would be those manufacturing or developing the products or involved in administration but without being seen by customers. Although the operations of a Back office are usually not given a lot of consideration, they are a major contributor to a business.
Front office	Front office is a business term that refers to a company`s departments that come in contact with clients, including the marketing, sales, and service departments. The Front office welcomes guests to the accommodation section: meeting and greeting them, taking and organizing reservations, allocating check in and out of rooms, organizing porter service, issuing keys and other security arrangements, passing on messages to customers and settling the accounts.
Outsourcing	Outsourcing often refers to the process of contracting to a third-party. While Outsourcing may be viewed as a component to the growing division of labor encompassing all societies, the term did not enter the English-speaking lexicon until the 1980s. Since the 1980s, transnational corporations have increased subcontracting across national boundaries.
Supply network	A Supply network is a pattern of temporal and spatial processes carried out at facility nodes and over distribution links, which adds value for customers through the manufacturing and delivery of products. It comprises the general state of business affairs in which all kinds of material are transformed and moved between various value-add points to maximize the value added for customers. A supply chain is a special instance of a Supply network in which raw materials, intermediate materials and finished goods are procured exclusively as products through a chain of processes that supply one another.
Hotel	A Hotel is an establishment that provides paid lodging on a short-term basis. The provision of basic accommodation, in times past, consisting only of a room with a bed, a cupboard, a small table and a washstand has largely been replaced by rooms with modern facilities, including en-suite bathrooms and air conditioning or climate control. Additional common features found in Hotel rooms are a telephone, an alarm clock, a television, and Internet connectivity; snack foods and drinks may be supplied in a mini-bar, and facilities for making hot drinks.

Chapter 2. operations, strategy and operations strategy

Trade-off	A Trade-off is a situation that involves losing one quality or aspect of something in return for gaining another quality or aspect. It implies a decision to be made with full comprehension of both the upside and downside of a particular choice.
	In economics the term is expressed as opportunity cost, referring to the most preferred alternative given up.
Performance measurement	Performance measurement is the process whereby an organization establishes the parameters within which programs, investments, and acquisitions are reaching the desired results.
	This process of measuring performance often requires the use of statistical evidence to determine progress toward specific defined organizational objectives.
Top-down	Top-down and bottom-up are strategies of information processing and knowledge ordering, mostly involving software, but also other humanistic and scientific theories . In practice, they can be seen as a style of thinking and teaching. In many cases top-down is used as a synonym of analysis or decomposition, and bottom-up of synthesis.
Infrastructure	Infrastructure is the basic physical and organizational structures needed for the operation of a society or enterprise, or the services and facilities necessary for an economy to function. The term typically refers to the technical structures that support a society, such as roads, water supply, sewers, power grids, telecommunications, and so forth. Viewed functionally, Infrastructure facilitates the production of goods and services; for example, roads enable the transport of raw materials to a factory, and also for the distribution of finished products to markets.

Chapter 3. The internationalization processes: drivers, challenges and benefits

Internationalization	In economics, Internationalization has been viewed as a process of increasing involvement of enterprises in international markets, although there is no agreed definition of Internationalization or international entrepreneurship. There are several Internationalization theories which try to explain why there are international activities.
E-commerce	E-commerce consists of the buying and selling of products or services over electronic systems such as the Internet and other computer networks. The amount of trade conducted electronically has grown extraordinarily with widespread Internet usage. The use of commerce is conducted in this way, spurring and drawing on innovations in electronic funds transfer, supply chain management, Internet marketing, online transaction processing, electronic data interchange (EDI), inventory management systems, and automated data collection systems.
Globalization	Globalization describes a process by which regional economies, societies, and cultures have become integrated through a global network of communication, transportation, and trade. The term is sometimes used to refer specifically to economic Globalization: the integration of national economies into the international economy through trade, foreign direct investment, capital flows, migration, and the spread of technology. However, Globalization is usually recognized as being driven by a combination of economic, technological, sociocultural, political, and biological factors.
Disintermediation	In economics, Disintermediation is the removal of intermediaries in a supply chain: `cutting out the middleman`. Instead of going through traditional distribution channels, which had some type of intermediate (such as a distributor, wholesaler, broker, or agent), companies may now deal with every customer directly, for example via the Internet. One important factor is a drop in the cost of servicing customers directly.
Uppsala model	The Uppsala model is a theory that explains how firms gradually intensify their activities in foreign markets. It is similar to the POM model. The key features of both models are the following: firms first gain experience from the domestic market before they move to foreign markets; firms start their foreign operations from culturally and/or geographically close countries and move gradually to culturally and geographically more distant countries; firms start their foreign operations by using traditional exports and gradually move to using more intensive and demanding operation modes (sales subsidiaries etc).
Product	When a Product reaches the maturity stage of the Product life cycle, a company may choose to operate strategies to extend the life of the Product. If the Product is predicted to continue to be successful or an upgrade is soon to be released the company can use various methods to keep sales, else the Product will be left as is to continue to the decline stage.

Examples of extension strategies are:

· Discounted price

· Increased advertising

· Accessing another market abroad

Corporification

In pre-modern chemistry, Corporification was the practice of recovering spirits into the same body, or at least into a body nearly the same, as that which they had before their spiritualization.

Chapter 4. International operations strategies

Economies of scale	Economies of scale, in microeconomics, refers to the cost advantages that a business obtains due to expansion. There are factors that cause a producer's average cost per unit to fall as the scale of output is increased. `Economies of scale` is a long run concept and refers to reductions in unit cost as the size of a facility and the usage levels of other inputs increase.
Call option	A Call option is a financial contract between two parties, the buyer and the seller of this type of option. The buyer of the option has the right, but not the obligation to buy an agreed quantity of a particular commodity or financial instrument (the underlying) from the seller of the option at a certain time (the expiration date) for a certain price. The seller (or `writer`) is obligated to sell the commodity or financial instrument should the buyer so decide. The buyer pays a fee for this right.
Economies of scope	Economies of scope are conceptually similar to economies of scale. Whereas economies of scale primarily refer to efficiencies associated with supply-side changes, such as increasing or decreasing the scale of production, of a single product type, Economies of scope refer to efficiencies primarily associated with demand-side changes, such as increasing or decreasing the scope of marketing and distribution, of different types of products. Economies of scope are one of the main reasons for such marketing strategies as product bundling, product lining, and family branding.
Mass customization	Mass customization, in marketing, manufacturing, call centres and management, is the use of flexible computer-aided manufacturing systems to produce custom output. Those systems combine the low unit costs of mass production processes with the flexibility of individual customization. Mass customization is the new frontier in business competition for both manufacturing and service industries.
Market access	Market access for goods in the WTO means the conditions, tariff and non-tariff measures, agreed by members for the entry of specific goods into their markets. Tariff commitments for goods are set out in each member's schedules of concessions on goods. The schedules represent commitments not to apply tariffs above the listed rates -- these rates are `bound`.
Resource	A Resource is any physical or virtual entity of limited availability that needs to be consumed to obtain a benefit from it. In most cases, commercial or even ethic factors require Resource allocation through Resource management.

Chapter 4. International operations strategies

Market entry	A Market entry strategy is the planned method of delivering goods or services to a target market and distributing them there. When importing or exporting services, it refers to establishing and managing contracts in a foreign country.
Joint venture	Some countries, such as the People's Republic of China and to some extent India, require foreign companies to form Joint ventures with domestic firms in order to enter a market. This requirement often forces technology transfers and managerial control to the domestic partner. In addition, Joint ventures are practiced by a Joint venture broker, who are people that often put together the two parties that participate in a Joint venture. A Joint venture broker then often make a percentage of the profit that is made from the deal between the two parties.
Subsidiary	A subsidiary, in business matters, is an entity that is controlled by a separate entity. The controlled entity is called a company, corporation, or limited liability company and in some cases can be a government or state-owned enterprise, and the controlling entity is called its parent (or the parent company). The reason for this distinction is that a lone company cannot be a subsidiary of any organization; only an entity representing a legal fiction as a separate entity can be a subsidiary.
GNI per capita	GNI per capita is the dollar value of a country's final income in a year (Gross National Income), divided by its population. It reflects the average income of a country's citizens. Knowing a country's GNI per capita is a good first step toward understanding the country's economic strengths and needs, as well as the general standard of living enjoyed by the average citizen. A country's GNI per capita tends to be closely linked with other indicators that measure the social, economic, and environmental well-being of the country and its people.
Competitive advantage	Competitive advantage is a position of a company in a competitive landscape that allows the company earning return on investments higher than the cost of investments. Competitive advantage should be relevant, unique, and sustainable.
Global sourcing	Global sourcing is a term used to describe practice of sourcing from the global market for goods and services across geopolitical boundaries. Global sourcing often aims to exploit global efficiencies in the delivery of a product or service. These efficiencies include low cost skilled labor, low cost raw material and other economic factors like tax breaks and low trade tariffs.
Network effect	In economics and business, a Network effect is the effect that one user of a good or service has on the value of that product to other people. When Network effect is present, the value of a product or service increases as more people use it.

Chapter 5. Facilities

Product	When a Product reaches the maturity stage of the Product life cycle, a company may choose to operate strategies to extend the life of the Product. If the Product is predicted to continue to be successful or an upgrade is soon to be released the company can use various methods to keep sales, else the Product will be left as is to continue to the decline stage.
	Examples of extension strategies are:
	· Discounted price
	· Increased advertising
	· Accessing another market abroad
Marketing	Marketing is the process by which companies create customer interest in goods or services. It generates the strategy that underlies sales techniques, business communication, and business developments. It is an integrated process through which companies build strong customer relationships and create value for their customers and for themselves.
Role	A Role or a social Role is a set of connected behaviors, rights and obligations as conceptualized by actors in a social situation. It is an expected or free or continuously changing behavior and may have a given individual social status or social position. It is vital to both functionalist and interactionist understandings of society. Social Role posits the following about social behavior:
	· The division of labor in society takes the form of the interaction among heterogeneous specialized positions, we call Roles.
	· Social Roles included appropriate and permitted forms of behavior, guided by social norms, which are commonly known and hence determine the expectations for appropriate behavior in these Roles.
	· Roles are occupied by individuals, who are called actors.
	· When individuals approve of a social Role they will incur costs to conform to Role norms, and will also incur costs to punish those who violate Role norms.
	· Changed conditions can render a social Role outdated or illegitimate, in which case social pressures are likely to lead to Role change

· The anticipation of rewards and punishments, as well as the satisfaction of behaving prosocially, account for why agents conform to Role requirements.

CᴸamΊΟΙ

Chapter 6. Capacity

Demand	In economics, Demand is the desire to own anything and the ability to pay for it and willingness to pay . The term Demand signifies the ability or the willingness to buy a particular commodity at a given point of time.
Forecasting	Forecasting is the process of estimation in unknown situations. Prediction is a similar, but more general term. Both can refer to estimation of time series, cross-sectional or longitudinal data.
Performance measurement	Performance measurement is the process whereby an organization establishes the parameters within which programs, investments, and acquisitions are reaching the desired results. This process of measuring performance often requires the use of statistical evidence to determine progress toward specific defined organizational objectives.
Time series	In statistics, signal processing, econometrics and mathematical finance, a Time series is a sequence of data points, measured typically at successive times spaced at uniform time intervals. Examples of Time series are the daily closing value of the Dow Jones index or the annual flow volume of the Nile River at Aswan. Time series analysis comprises methods for analyzing Time series data in order to extract meaningful statistics and other characteristics of the data.
Time series analysis	In statistics, signal processing, and many other fields, a time series is a sequence of data points, measured typically at successive times, spaced at (often uniform) time intervals. Time series analysis comprises methods that attempt to understand such time series, often either to understand the underlying context of the data points (Where did they come from? What generated them?), or to make forecasts (predictions.) Time series forecasting is the use of a model to forecast future events based on known past events: to forecast future data points before they are measured.
Scenario planning	Scenario planning is a strategic planning method that some organizations use to make flexible long-term plans. It is in large part an adaptation and generalization of classic methods used by military intelligence.
Capacity management	Capacity management is a process used to manage information technology (IT). Its primary goal is to ensure that IT capacity meets current and future business requirements in a cost-effective manner. One common interpretation of Capacity management is described in the ITIL framework.

Chapter 6. Capacity

Customer	A Customer is usually used to refer to a current or potential buyer or user of the products of an individual or organization, called the supplier, seller, or vendor. This is typically through purchasing or renting goods or services. However, in certain contexts, the term Customer also includes by extension any entity that uses or experiences the services of another.
Part-time	A Part-time job is a form of employment that carries fewer hours per week than a full-time job. Workers are considered to be Part-time if they commonly work fewer than 30 or 35 hours per week. According to the International Labour Organization, the number of Part-time workers has increased from one-fourth to a half in the past 20 years in most developed countries, excluding the United States. There are many reasons for working Part-time, including the desire to do so, having one`s hours cut back by an employer and being unable to find a full-time job.
Peak demand	Peak demand is used to refer to a historically high point in the sales record of a particular product. In terms of energy use, Peak demand describes a period of strong consumer demand.
Workforce	The Workforce is the labor pool in employment. It is generally used to describe those working for a single company or industry, but can also apply to a geographic region like a city, country, state, etc. The term generally excludes the employers or management, and implies those involved in manual labor.
Activity-based costing	Activity-based costing is a costing model that identifies activities in an organization and assigns the cost of each activity resource to all products and services according to the actual consumption by each: it assigns more indirect costs (overhead) into direct costs. In this way an organization can precisely estimate the cost of its individual products and services for the purposes of identifying and eliminating those which are unprofitable and lowering the prices of those which are overpriced. In a business organization, the Activity based costing methodology assigns an organization`s resource costs through activities to the products and services provided to its customers.
ABC analysis	ABC analysis is a business term used to define an inventory categorization technique often used in materials management. It is also known as Selective Inventory Control.

Chapter 6. Capacity

Chapter 6. Capacity

	ABC analysis provides a mechanism for identifying items that will have a significant impact on overall inventory cost, whilst also providing a mechanism for identifying different categories of stock that will require different management and controls.
Construction aggregate	Construction aggregate is a broad category of coarse particulate material used in construction, including sand, gravel, crushed stone, slag, recycled concrete and geosynthetic aggregates. Aggregates are a component of composite materials such as concrete and asphalt concrete; the aggregate serves as reinforcement to add strength to the overall composite material. Due to the relatively high hydraulic conductivity value as compared to most soils, aggregates are widely used in drainage applications such as foundation and french drains, septic drain fields, retaining wall drains, and road side edge drains.
Customer service	Customer service is the provision of service to customers before, during and after a purchase.
	According to Jamier L. Scott. (2002), `Customer service is a series of activities designed to enhance the level of customer satisfaction - that is, the feeling that a product or service has met the customer expectation.`
	Its importance varies by product, industry and customer; defective or broken merchandise can be exchanged, often only with a receipt and within a specified time frame. Retail stores will often have a desk or counter devoted to dealing with returns, exchanges and complaints, or will perform related functions at the point of sale.
Demand management	Demand management is a planning methodology use to manage forecasted demand.
	In economics, Demand management is the art or science of controlling economic demand to avoid a recession. In natural resources management and environmental policy more generally, it refers to policies to control consumer demand for environmentally sensitive or harmful goods such as water and energy.
Pricing	Pricing is the process of determining what a company will receive in exchange for its products. Pricing factors are manufacturing cost, market place, competition, market condition, and quality of product. Pricing is also a key variable in microeconomic price allocation theory.

Chapter 6. Capacity

Promotion	Promotion is one of the four elements of marketing mix . It is the communication link between sellers and buyers for the purpose of influencing, informing, or persuading a potential buyer's purchasing decision. The following are two types of Promotion: · Above the line Promotion: Promotion in the media in which the advertiser pays an advertising agency to place the ad · Below the line Promotion: All other Promotion. Much of this is intended to be subtle enough for the consumer to be unaware that Promotion is taking place.
Discounting	Discounting is a financial mechanism in which a debtor obtains the right to delay payments to a creditor, for a defined period of time, in exchange for a charge or fee. Essentially, the party that owes money in the present purchases the right to delay the payment until some future date. The discount, or charge, is simply the difference between the original amount owed in the present and the amount that has to be paid in the future to settle the debt.
Price	In ordinary usage, Price is the quantity of payment or compensation given from one party to another in return for goods or services. In all modern economies, the overwhelming majority of Prices are quoted in (and the transactions involve) units of some form of currency. Although in theory, Prices could be quoted as quantities of other goods or services this sort of barter exchange is rarely seen.
Yield management	Yield management is the process of understanding, anticipating and influencing consumer behavior in order to maximize revenue or profits from a fixed, perishable resource (such as airline seats or hotel room reservations). The challenge is to sell the right resources to the right customer at the right time for the right price. This process can result in price discrimination, where a firm charges customers consuming otherwise identical goods or services a different price for doing so.
Overbooking	Overbooking is a term used to describe the sale of access to a service which exceeds the capacity of the service.

Chapter 6. Capacity

Hotel	A Hotel is an establishment that provides paid lodging on a short-term basis. The provision of basic accommodation, in times past, consisting only of a room with a bed, a cupboard, a small table and a washstand has largely been replaced by rooms with modern facilities, including en-suite bathrooms and air conditioning or climate control. Additional common features found in Hotel rooms are a telephone, an alarm clock, a television, and Internet connectivity; snack foods and drinks may be supplied in a mini-bar, and facilities for making hot drinks.

Chapter 7. Process technology

Customer	A Customer is usually used to refer to a current or potential buyer or user of the products of an individual or organization, called the supplier, seller, or vendor. This is typically through purchasing or renting goods or services. However, in certain contexts, the term Customer also includes by extension any entity that uses or experiences the services of another.
Interaction	Interaction is a kind of action that occurs as two or more objects have an effect upon one another. The idea of a two-way effect is essential in the concept of Interaction, as opposed to a one-way causal effect. A c osely related term is interconnectivity, which deals with the Interactions of Interactions within systems: combinations of many simple Interactions can lead to surprising emergent phenomena.
Electronic business	Electronic business may be defined as the utilization of information and communication technologies (ICT) in support of all the activities of business. Commerce constitutes the exchange of products and services between businesses, groups and individuals and can be seen as one of the essential activities of any business. Electronic commerce focuses on the use of ICT to enable the external activities and relationships of the business with individuals, groups and other businesses.
E-commerce	E-commerce consists of the buying and selling of products or services over electronic systems such as the Internet and other computer networks. The amount of trade conducted electronically has grown extraordinarily with widespread Internet usage. The use of commerce is conducted in this way, spurring and drawing on innovations in electronic funds transfer, supply chain management, Internet marketing, online transaction processing, electronic data interchange (EDI), inventory management systems, and automated data collection systems.
Taguchi methods	Taguchi methods are statistical methods developed by Genichi Taguchi to improve the quality of manufactured goods, and more recently also applied to, engineering, biotechnology, marketing and advertising. Professional statisticians have welcomed the goals and improvements brought about by Taguchi methods, particularly by Taguchi`s development of designs for studying variation, but have criticized the inefficiency of some of Taguchi`s proposals.
Automation	Automation is the use of control systems and information technologies reducing the need for human intervention. In the scope of industrialization, Automation is a step beyond mechanization. Whereas mechanization provided human operators with machinery to assist them with the muscular requirements of work, Automation greatly reduces the need for human sensory and mental requirements as well.

Chapter 7. Process technology

Information and communication technologies	Information and communication technologies is an umbrella term that covers all technical means for processing and communicating information. While this technically encompasses pre-digital technologies, including paper-based writing, it is most often used to describe digital technologies including methods for communication (communication protocols, transmission techniques, communications equipment, media (communication)), as well as techniques for storing and processing information (computing, data storage, etc). The term has gained popularity partially due to the convergence of information technology (IT) and telecom technology.
Role	A Role or a social Role is a set of connected behaviors, rights and obligations as conceptualized by actors in a social situation. It is an expected or free or continuously changing behavior and may have a given individual social status or social position. It is vital to both functionalist and interactionist understandings of society. Social Role posits the following about social behavior: · The division of labor in society takes the form of the interaction among heterogeneous specialized positions, we call Roles. · Social Roles included appropriate and permitted forms of behavior, guided by social norms, which are commonly known and hence determine the expectations for appropriate behavior in these Roles. · Roles are occupied by individuals, who are called actors. · When individuals approve of a social Role they will incur costs to conform to Role norms, and will also incur costs to punish those who violate Role norms. · Changed conditions can render a social Role outdated or illegitimate, in which case social pressures are likely to lead to Role change · The anticipation of rewards and punishments, as well as the satisfaction of behaving prosocially, account for why agents conform to Role requirements.
Business process	A Business process or business method is a collection of related, structured activities or tasks that produce a specific service or product for a particular customer or customers. It often can be visualized with a flowchart as a sequence of activities. There are three types of Business processes: · Management processes, the processes that govern the operation of a system. Typical management processes include `Corporate Governance` and `Strategic Management`.

Chapter 7. Process technology

· Operational processes, processes that constitute the core business and create the primary value stream. Typical operational processes are Purchasing, Manufacturing, Marketing and Sales.

· Supporting processes, which support the core processes. Examples include Accounting, Recruitment, Technical support.

Business process redesign	Business process reengineering is, in management, an approach aiming at improvements by means of elevating efficiency and effectiveness of the business process that exist within and across organizations. The key to Business process redesign is for organizations to look at their business processes from a `clean slate` perspective and determine how they can best construct these processes to improve how they conduct business.
Technology transfer	Technology transfer is the process of sharing of skills, knowledge, technologies, methods of manufacturing, samples of manufacturing and facilities among governments and other institutions to ensure that scientific and technological developments are accessible to a wider range of users who can then further develop and exploit the technology into new products, processes, applications, materials or services. It is closely related to (and may arguably be considered a subset of) knowledge transfer. Technology brokers are people who discovered how to bridge the disparate worlds and apply scientific concepts or processes to new situations or circumstances.
Job production	Job production involves producing a one-off product for a specific customer. Job production is most often associated with small firms (making railings for a specific house, building/repairing a computer for a specific customer, making flower arrangements for a specific wedding etc). but large firms use Job production too. Examples include:

· Designing and implementing an advertising campaign

· Auditing the accounts of a large public limited company

· Building a new factory

· Installing machinery in a factory

· Machining a batch of parts per a CAD drawing supplied by a customer

Fabrication shops and machine shops whose work is primarily of the Job production type are often called job shops.

Continuous

In probability theory, a probability distribution is called continuous if its cumulative distribution function is continuous . This is equivalent to saying that for random variables X with the distribution in question, Pr[X = a] = 0 for all real numbers a, i.e.: the probability that X attains the value a is zero, for any number a. If the distribution of X is continuous then X is called a continuous random variable.

Marking out

Marking out is the process of transferring a design or pattern to a workpiece, as the first step in the manufacturing process. It is performed in many industries or hobbies although in the repetition industries the machine`s initial setup is designed to remove the need to mark out every individual piece.

Product

When a Product reaches the maturity stage of the Product life cycle, a company may choose to operate strategies to extend the life of the Product. If the Product is predicted to continue to be successful or an upgrade is soon to be released the company can use various methods to keep sales, else the Product will be left as is to continue to the decline stage.

Examples of extension strategies are:

· Discounted price

· Increased advertising

· Accessing another market abroad

Chapter 8. The supply network

Supply chain	A Supply chain is a system of organizations, people, technology, activities, information and resources involved in moving a product or service from supplier to customer. Supply chain activities transform natural resources, raw materials and components into a finished product that is delivered to the end customer. In sophisticated Supply chain systems, used products may re-enter the Supply chain at any point where residual value is recyclable.
Performance measurement	Performance measurement is the process whereby an organization establishes the parameters within which programs, investments, and acquisitions are reaching the desired results. This process of measuring performance often requires the use of statistical evidence to determine progress toward specific defined organizational objectives.
Outsourcing	Outsourcing often refers to the process of contracting to a third-party. While Outsourcing may be viewed as a component to the growing division of labor encompassing all societies, the term did not enter the English-speaking lexicon until the 1980s. Since the 1980s, transnational corporations have increased subcontracting across national boundaries.
Product	When a Product reaches the maturity stage of the Product life cycle, a company may choose to operate strategies to extend the life of the Product. If the Product is predicted to continue to be successful or an upgrade is soon to be released the company can use various methods to keep sales, else the Product will be left as is to continue to the decline stage. Examples of extension strategies are: · Discounted price · Increased advertising · Accessing another market abroad
Vertical integration	In microeconomics and management, the term Vertical integration describes a style of management control. Vertically integrated companies in a supply chain are united through a common owner. Usually each member of the supply chain produces a different product or (market-specific) service, and the products combine to satisfy a common need.

Chapter 8. The supply network

Competence	Competence is the ability to perform a specific task, action or function successfully. Competence, in human resource is a standardized requirement for an individual to properly perform a specific job
Global sourcing	Global sourcing is a term used to describe practice of sourcing from the global market for goods and services across geopolitical boundaries. Global sourcing often aims to exploit global efficiencies in the delivery of a product or service. These efficiencies include low cost skilled labor, low cost raw material and other economic factors like tax breaks and low trade tariffs.
Supply network	A Supply network is a pattern of temporal and spatial processes carried out at facility nodes and over distribution links, which adds value for customers through the manufacturing and delivery of products. It comprises the general state of business affairs in which all kinds of material are transformed and moved between various value-add points to maximize the value added for customers. A supply chain is a special instance of a Supply network in which raw materials, intermediate materials and finished goods are procured exclusively as products through a chain of processes that supply one another.

Chapter 9. Planning and Control

Resource	A Resource is any physical or virtual entity of limited availability that needs to be consumed to obtain a benefit from it. In most cases, commercial or even ethic factors require Resource allocation through Resource management.
Activity-based costing	Activity-based costing is a costing model that identifies activities in an organization and assigns the cost of each activity resource to all products and services according to the actual consumption by each: it assigns more indirect costs (overhead) into direct costs.
	In this way an organization can precisely estimate the cost of its individual products and services for the purposes of identifying and eliminating those which are unprofitable and lowering the prices of those which are overpriced.
	In a business organization, the Activity based costing methodology assigns an organization`s resource costs through activities to the products and services provided to its customers.
ABC analysis	ABC analysis is a business term used to define an inventory categorization technique often used in materials management. It is also known as Selective Inventory Control.
	ABC analysis provides a mechanism for identifying items that will have a significant impact on overall inventory cost, whilst also providing a mechanism for identifying different categories of stock that will require different management and controls.
Construction aggregate	Construction aggregate is a broad category of coarse particulate material used in construction, including sand, gravel, crushed stone, slag, recycled concrete and geosynthetic aggregates. Aggregates are a component of composite materials such as concrete and asphalt concrete; the aggregate serves as reinforcement to add strength to the overall composite material. Due to the relatively high hydraulic conductivity value as compared to most soils, aggregates are widely used in drainage applications such as foundation and french drains, septic drain fields, retaining wall drains, and road side edge drains.
Aggregate planning	Aggregate planning is an operational activity that does an aggregate plan for the production process, in advance of 2 to 18 months, to give an idea to management as to what quantity of materials and other resources are to be procured and when, so that the total cost of operations of the organization is kept to the minimum over that period.

	The quantity of outsourcing, subcontracting of items, overtime of labour, numbers to be hired and fired in each period and the amount of inventory to be held in stock and to be backlogged for each period are decided. All of these activities are done within the framework of the company ethics, policies, and long term commitment to the society, community and the country of operation.
Production scheduling	Scheduling is an important tool for manufacturing and engineering, where it can have a major impact on the productivity of a process. In manufacturing, the purpose of scheduling is to minimize the production time and costs, by telling a production facility what to make, when, with which staff, and on which equipment. Production scheduling aims to maximize the efficiency of the operation and reduce costs.
Customer	A Customer is usually used to refer to a current or potential buyer or user of the products of an individual or organization, called the supplier, seller, or vendor. This is typically through purchasing or renting goods or services. However, in certain contexts, the term Customer also includes by extension any entity that uses or experiences the services of another.
Demand	In economics, Demand is the desire to own anything and the ability to pay for it and willingness to pay . The term Demand signifies the ability or the willingness to buy a particular commodity at a given point of time.
Expediting	Expediting is a concept in purchasing and project management for securing the quality and timely delivery of goods and components.
	The procurement department or an external expediter controls the progress of manufacturing at the supplier concerning quality, packing, conformity with standards and set timelines. Thus the expediter makes sure that the required goods arrive at the appointed date in the agreed quality at the agreed location.
Postponement	Postponement is a business strategy that maximizes possible benefit and minimizes risk by delaying further investment into a product or service until the last possible moment. An example of this strategy is Dell Computers` build-to-order online store.
Inventory	Inventory is a list for goods and materials, or those goods and materials themselves, held available in stock by a business. It is also used for a list of the contents of a household and for a list for testamentary purposes of the possessions of someone who has died. In accounting Inventory is considered an asset.

Chapter 9. Planning and Control

Independent	In probability theory, to say that two events are independent intuitively means that the occurrence of one event makes it neither more nor less probable that the other occurs. For example:
	· The event of getting a 6 the first time a die is rolled and the event of getting a 6 the second time are independent
	· By contrast, the event of getting a 6 the first time a die is rolled and the event that the sum of the numbers seen on the first and second trials is 8 are dependent
	· If two cards are drawn with replacement from a deck of cards, the event of drawing a red card on the first trial and that of drawing a red card on the second trial are independent
	· By contrast, if two cards are drawn without replacement from a deck of cards, the event of drawing a red card on the first trial and that of drawing a red card on the second trial are dependent
	Similarly, two random variables are independent if the conditional probability distribution of either given the observed value of the other is the same as if the other`s value had not been observed. The concept of independence extends to dealing with collections of more than two events or random variables.
	In some instances, the term `independent` is replaced by `statistically independent`, `marginally independent`, or `absolutely independent`.
Control system	A Control system is a device or set of devices to manage, command, direct or regulate the behavior of other devices or systems.
	There are two common classes of Control systems, with many variations and combinations: logic or sequential controls, and feedback or linear controls. There is also fuzzy logic, which attempts to combine some of the design simplicity of logic with the utility of linear control.
Inventory control system	An Inventory control system is a process for keeping track of objects or materials. In common usage, the term may also refer to just the software components.

Modern Inventory control systems rely upon barcodes, and potentially RFID tags, to provide automatic identification of inventory objects.

Lean manufacturing	Lean manufacturing is a production practice that considers the expenditure of resources for any goal other than the creation of value for the end customer to be wasteful, and thus a target for elimination. Working from the perspective of the customer who consumes a product or service, `value` is defined as any action or process that a customer would be willing to pay for. Basically, lean is centered on preserving value with less work.

Chapter 10. Quality

Deming Prize	The Deming Prize, established in December 1950 in honor of W. Edwards Deming, was originally designed to reward Japanese companies for major advances in quality improvement. Over the years it has grown, under the guidance of Japanese Union of Scientists and Engineers to where it is now also available to non-Japanese companies, albeit usually operating in Japan, and also to individuals recognized as having made major contributions to the advancement of quality. The awards ceremony is broadcast every year in Japan on national television.
Cost	In business, retail, and accounting, a Cost is the value of money that has been used up to produce something, and hence is not available for use anymore. In economics, a Cost is an alternative that is given up as a result of a decision. In business, the Cost may be one of acquisition, in which case the amount of money expended to acquire it is counted as Cost.
G-code	G-code are functions in the Numerical control programming language. The G-codes are the codes that position the tool and do the actual work, as opposed to M-codes, that manages the machine, T for tool-related codes. S and F are tool-Speed and tool-Feed, and finally D-codes for tool compensation.
Quality assurance	Quality assurance refers to a program for the systematic monitoring and evaluation of the various aspects of a project, service, or facility to ensure that standards of quality are being met. It is important to realize also that quality is determined by the program sponsor. Quality assurance cannot absolutely guarantee the production of quality products, unfortunately, but makes this more likely.
Quality control	Quality control is a process by which entities review the quality of all factors involved in production. This approach places an emphasis on three aspects: · Elements such as controls, job management, defined and well managed processes, performance and integrity criteria, and identification of records · Competence, such as knowledge, skills, experience, and qualifications · Soft elements, such as personnel integrity, confidence, organizational culture, motivation, team spirit, and quality relationships.

The quality of the outputs is at risk if any of these three aspects is deficient in any way. Quality control emphasizes testing of products to uncover defects, and reporting to management who make the decision to allow or deny the release, whereas quality assurance attempts to improve and stabilize production, and associated processes, to avoid, or at least minimize, issues that led to the defects in the first place.

Quality circle

A Quality circle is a volunteer group composed of workers (or even students), usually under the leadership of their supervisor (but they can elect a team leader), who are trained to identify, analyse and solve work-related problems and present their solutions to management in order to improve the performance of the organization, and motivate and enrich the work of employees. When matured, true Quality circles become self-managing, having gained the confidence of management.

Competence

Competence is the ability to perform a specific task, action or function successfully. Competence, in human resource is a standardized requirement for an individual to properly perform a specific job

Customer

A Customer is usually used to refer to a current or potential buyer or user of the products of an individual or organization, called the supplier, seller, or vendor. This is typically through purchasing or renting goods or services. However, in certain contexts, the term Customer also includes by extension any entity that uses or experiences the services of another.

Value-based

Value-based pricing is dependent upon an understanding of how customers measure value, through careful evaluation of customer operations. Survey methods are sometimes used to determine the value, and therefore the willingness to pay, a customer attributes to a product or a service. Frameworks for value-based procing include Economic Value Estimation are Relative Attribute Positioning, Van Westendorp Price Sensitivly Meter, Conjoint Analysis and Navetti Ratio To Complete.

Quality function deployment

Quality function deployment is a `method to transform user demands into design quality, to deploy the functions forming quality, and to deploy methods for achieving the design quality into subsystems and component parts, and ultimately to specific elements of the manufacturing process.` , as described by Dr. Yoji Akao, who originally developed Quality function deployment in Japan in 1966, when the author combined his work in quality assurance and quality control points with function deployment used in Value Engineering.

Quality function deployment is designed to help planners focus on characteristics of a new or existing product or service from the viewpoints of market segments, company, or technology-development needs. The technique yields graphs and matrices.

Chapter 10. Quality

Activity-based costing	Activity-based costing is a costing model that identifies activities in an organization and assigns the cost of each activity resource to all products and services according to the actual consumption by each: it assigns more indirect costs (overhead) into direct costs.
	In this way an organization can precisely estimate the cost of its individual products and services for the purposes of identifying and eliminating those which are unprofitable and lowering the prices of those which are overpriced.
	In a business organization, the Activity based costing methodology assigns an organization`s resource costs through activities to the products and services provided to its customers.
ABC analysis	ABC analysis is a business term used to define an inventory categorization technique often used in materials management. It is also known as Selective Inventory Control.
	ABC analysis provides a mechanism for identifying items that will have a significant impact on overall inventory cost, whilst also providing a mechanism for identifying different categories of stock that will require different management and controls.
Acceptance sampling	Acceptance sampling uses statistical sampling to determine whether to accept or reject a production lot of material. It has been a common quality control technique used in industry and particularly the military for contracts and procurement. A wide variety of Acceptance sampling plans are avilable.
Control chart	Control charts in statistical process control are tools used to determine whether or not a manufacturing or business process is in a state of statistical control.
	If analysis of the Control chart indicates that the process is currently under control then data from the process can be used to predict the future performance of the process. If the chart indicates that the process being monitored is not in control, analysis of the chart can help determine the sources of variation, which can then be eliminated to bring the process back into control.
Process control	Process control is a statistics and engineering discipline that deals with architectures, mechanisms, and algorithms for controlling the output of a specific process.

Chapter 10. Quality

Statistical process control	Statistical process control is the application of statistical methods to the monitoring and control of a process to ensure that it operates at its full potential to produce conforming product. Under Statistical process control, a process behaves predictably to produce as much conforming product as possible with the least possible waste. While Statistical process control has been applied most frequently to controlling manufacturing lines, it applies equally well to any process with a measurable output. Key tools in Statistical process control are control charts, a focus on continuous improvement and designed experiments.
Quality management	Quality management can be considered to have three main components: quality control, quality assurance and quality improvement. Quality management is focused not only on product/service quality, but also the means to achieve it. Quality management therefore uses quality assurance and control of processes as well as products to achieve more consistent quality.
Total quality management	Total quality management is a management concept coined by W. Edwards Deming. The basis of Total quality management is to reduce the errors produced during the manufacturing or service process, increase customer satisfaction, streamline supply chain management, aim for modernization of equipment and ensure workers have the highest level of training. One of the principal aims of Total quality management is to limit errors to 1 per 1 million units produced. Total quality management is often associated with the development, deployment, and maintenance of organizational systems that are required for various business processes.
Six Sigma	Six Sigma is a business management strategy originally developed by Motorola, USA in 1981. As of 2010, it enjoys widespread application in many sectors of industry, although its application is not without controversy. Six Sigma seeks to improve the quality of process outputs by identifying and removing the causes of defects (errors) and minimizing variability in manufacturing and business processes. It uses a set of quality management methods, including statistical methods, and creates a special infrastructure of people within the organization (`Black Belts`, `Green Belts`, etc). who are experts in these methods. Each Six Sigma project carried out within an organization follows a defined sequence of steps and has quantified targets. These targets can be financial or whatever is critical to the customer of that process (cycle time, safety, delivery, etc.).

Chapter 11. Work organization

Centralization	Centralization is the process by which the activities of an organization, particularly those regarding Planing decision-making, become concentrated within a particular location and/or group.
Division of labour	Division of labour is the specialization of cooperative labour in specific, circumscribed tasks and roles. Historically an increasingly complex division of labor is closely associated with the growth of total output and trade, the rise of capitalism, and of the complexity of industrialization processes. Division of labor was also a method used by the neolithics and paleolithics to categorize different jobs, and divide them to skilled members of a society.
Economic value	The Economic value of a good or service has puzzled economists since the beginning of the discipline. First, economists tried to estimate the value of a good to an individual alone, and extend that definition to goods which can be exchanged. From this analysis came the concepts value in use and value in exchange.Wealth maximization predicts that a person will choose to obtain the good or service in the place where it is cheapest, where the amount given up is the least.Value is linked to price through the mechanism of exchange. When an economist observes an exchange, two important value functions are revealed: those of the buyer and seller. Just as the buyer reveals what he is willing to pay for a certain amount of a good, so too does the seller reveal what it costs him to give up the good.
Organizational culture	Organizational culture is an idea in the field of Organizational studies and management which describes the psychology, attitudes, experiences, beliefs and values (personal and cultural values) of an organization. It has been defined as `the specific collection of values and norms that are shared by people and groups in an organization and that control the way they interact with each other and with stakeholders outside the organization.` This definition continues to explain organizational values, also known as `beliefs and ideas about what kinds of goals members of an organization should pursue and ideas about the appropriate kinds or standards of behavior organizational members should use to achieve these goals. From organizational values develop organizational norms, guidelines, or expectations that prescribe appropriate kinds of behavior by employees in particular situations and control the behavior of organizational members towards one another.`

Chapter 11. Work organization

Role	A Role or a social Role is a set of connected behaviors, rights and obligations as conceptualized by actors in a social situation. It is an expected or free or continuously changing behavior and may have a given individual social status or social position. It is vital to both functionalist and interactionist understandings of society. Social Role posits the following about social behavior: · The division of labor in society takes the form of the interaction among heterogeneous specialized positions, we call Roles. · Social Roles included appropriate and permitted forms of behavior, guided by social norms, which are commonly known and hence determine the expectations for appropriate behavior in these Roles. · Roles are occupied by individuals, who are called actors. · When individuals approve of a social Role they will incur costs to conform to Role norms, and will also incur costs to punish those who violate Role norms. · Changed conditions can render a social Role outdated or illegitimate, in which case social pressures are likely to lead to Role change · The anticipation of rewards and punishments, as well as the satisfaction of behaving prosocially, account for why agents conform to Role requirements.
Interaction	Interaction is a kind of action that occurs as two or more objects have an effect upon one another. The idea of a two-way effect is essential in the concept of Interaction, as opposed to a one-way causal effect. A closely related term is interconnectivity, which deals with the Interactions of Interactions within systems: combinations of many simple Interactions can lead to surprising emergent phenomena.
Time horizon	A Time horizon is a fixed point of time in the future at which point certain processes will be evaluated or assumed to end. It is necessary in an accounting, finance or risk management regime to assign such a fixed horizon time so that alternatives can be evaluated for performance over the same period of time. A Time horizon is a physical impossibility in the real world.
GNI per capita	GNI per capita is the dollar value of a country`s final income in a year (Gross National Income), divided by its population. It reflects the average income of a country`s citizens.

Chapter 11. Work organization

Knowing a country`s GNI per capita is a good first step toward understanding the country`s economic strengths and needs, as well as the general standard of living enjoyed by the average citizen. A country`s GNI per capita tends to be closely linked with other indicators that measure the social, economic, and environmental well-being of the country and its people.

Taguchi methods	Taguchi methods are statistical methods developed by Genichi Taguchi to improve the quality of manufactured goods, and more recently also applied to, engineering, biotechnology, marketing and advertising. Professional statisticians have welcomed the goals and improvements brought about by Taguchi methods, particularly by Taguchi`s development of designs for studying variation, but have criticized the inefficiency of some of Taguchi`s proposals.
Empowerment	Empowerment refers to increasing the spiritual, political, social, or economic strength of individuals and communities. It often involves the empowered developing confidence in their own capacities.
	The term Empowerment covers a vast landscape of meanings, interpretations, definitions and disciplines ranging from psychology and philosophy to the highly commercialized self-help industry and motivational sciences.
Quality circle	A Quality circle is a volunteer group composed of workers (or even students), usually under the leadership of their supervisor (but they can elect a team leader), who are trained to identify, analyse and solve work-related problems and present their solutions to management in order to improve the performance of the organization, and motivate and enrich the work of employees. When matured, true Quality circles become self-managing, having gained the confidence of management.
Cross-functional team	A cross-functional team is a group of employees from various functional areas of the organization - research, engineering, marketing, finance, human resources, and operations, for example - who are all focused on a specific objective and are responsible to work as a team to improve coordination and innovation across divisions and resolve mutual problems.
Product	When a Product reaches the maturity stage of the Product life cycle, a company may choose to operate strategies to extend the life of the Product. If the Product is predicted to continue to be successful or an upgrade is soon to be released the company can use various methods to keep sales, else the Product will be left as is to continue to the decline stage.

Examples of extension strategies are:

· Discounted price

· Increased advertising

· Accessing another market abroad

Virtual team

A Virtual team -- also known as a geographically dispersed team (GDT) -- is a group of individuals who work across time, space, and organizational boundaries with links strengthened by webs of communication technology. Members of Virtual teams communicate electronically, so they may never meet face to face. Virtual teams are made possible by a proliferation of fiber optic technology that has significantly increased the scope of off-site communication.

Work design

In organizational development (OD), Work design is the application of Socio-Technical Systems principles and techniques to the humanization of work.

The aims of Work design to improved job satisfaction, to improved through-put, to improved quality and to reduced employee problems, e.g., grievances, absenteeism.

Under scientific management people would be directed by reason and the problems of industrial unrest would be appropriately (i.e., scientifically) addressed.

Groupthink

Groupthink is a type of thought within a deeply cohesive in-group whose members try to minimize conflict and reach consensus without critically testing, analyzing, and evaluating ideas. It is a second potential negative consequence of group cohesion.

Irving Janis studied a number of American Foreign policy `disasters` such as failure to anticipate the Japanese attack on Pearl Harbor ; the Bay of Pigs fiasco (1961) when the US adminstration sought to overthrow Cuban Government of Fidel Castro; and the prosecution of the Vietnam War (1964-67) by President Lyndon Johnson.

Workforce | The Workforce is the labor pool in employment. It is generally used to describe those working for a single company or industry, but can also apply to a geographic region like a city, country, state, etc. The term generally excludes the employers or management, and implies those involved in manual labor.

Chapter 12. Human resource management

Human resource management	Human resource management is the strategic and coherent approach to the management of an organization's most valued assets - the people working there who individually and collectively contribute to the achievement of the objectives of the business. The terms `Human resource management` and `human resources` (HR) have largely replaced the term `personnel management` as a description of the processes involved in managing people in organizations. In simple words, Human resource management means employing people, developing their capacities, utilizing, maintaining and compensating their services in tune with the job and organizational requirement. Its features include: · Organizational management · Personnel administration · Manpower management · Industrial management But these traditional expressions are becoming less common for the theoretical discipline.
Resource	A Resource is any physical or virtual entity of limited availability that needs to be consumed to obtain a benefit from it. In most cases, commercial or even ethic factors require Resource allocation through Resource management.
Job description	A Job description is a list of the general tasks, or functions, and responsibilities of a position. Typically, it also includes to whom the position reports, specifications such as the qualifications needed by the person in the job, salary range for the position, etc. A Job description is usually developed by conducting a job analysis, which includes examining the tasks and sequences of tasks necessary to perform the job.
Person specification	The Person specification is an extension of the job description. It is a profile of the type of person needed to do a job and is produced along with a job description following a job analysis.

Chapter 12. Human resource management

Recruitment	`Onboarding` is a term which describes the introduction or `induction` process. A well-planned introduction helps new employees become fully operational quickly and is often integrated with a new company and environment. Onboarding is included in the Recruitment process for retention purposes.
Human resources	Human resources is a term used to describe the individuals who comprise the workforce of an organization, although it is also applied in labor economics to, for example, business sectors or even whole nations. Human resources is also the name of the function within an organization charged with the overall responsibility for implementing strategies and policies relating to the management of individuals (i.e. the Human resources).
Training and development	In the field of human resource management, Training and development is the field concerned with organizational activity aimed at bettering the performance of individuals and groups in organizational settings. It has been known by several names, including employee development, human resource development, and learning and development.
E-learning	E-learning comprises all forms of electronically supported learning and teaching, which are procedural in character and aim to effect the construction of knowledge with reference to individual experience, practice and knowledge of the learner. Information and communication systems, whether networked or not, serve as specific media to implement the learning process. E-learning is essentially the computer and network enabled transfer of skills and knowledge.
Scientific management	Scientific management is a theory of management that analyzes and synthesizes workflows, with the objective of improving labor productivity. The core ideas of the theory were developed by Frederick Winslow Taylor in the 1880s and 1890s, and were first published in his monographs, Shop Management (1905) and The Principles of Scientific management. He began trying to discover a way for workers to increase their efficiency when he was the foreperson at the Midvale Steele Company in 1875. Taylor believed that decisions based upon tradition and rules of thumb should be replaced by precise procedures developed after careful study of an individual at work.
Activity-based costing	Activity-based costing is a costing model that identifies activities in an organization and assigns the cost of each activity resource to all products and services according to the actual consumption by each: it assigns more indirect costs (overhead) into direct costs.

In this way an organization can precisely estimate the cost of its individual products and services for the purposes of identifying and eliminating those which are unprofitable and lowering the prices of those which are overpriced.

In a business organization, the Activity based costing methodology assigns an organization`s resource costs through activities to the products and services provided to its customers.

ABC analysis	ABC analysis is a business term used to define an inventory categorization technique often used in materials management. It is also known as Selective Inventory Control.
	ABC analysis provides a mechanism for identifying items that will have a significant impact on overall inventory cost, whilst also providing a mechanism for identifying different categories of stock that will require different management and controls.
Performance measurement	Performance measurement is the process whereby an organization establishes the parameters within which programs, investments, and acquisitions are reaching the desired results.
	This process of measuring performance often requires the use of statistical evidence to determine progress toward specific defined organizational objectives.
Sampling	Sampling is that part of statistical practice concerned with the selection of an unbiased or random subset of individual observations within a population of individuals intended to yield some knowledge about the population of concern, especially for the purposes of making predictions based on statistical inference. Sampling is an important aspect of data collection.
	Researchers rarely survey the entire population for two reasons (Adèr, Mellenbergh, ' Hand, 2008): the cost is too high, and the population is dynamic in that the individuals making up the population may change over time.
Job enlargement	Job enlargement means increasing the scope of a job through extending the range of its job duties and responsibilities. This contradicts the principles of specialisation and the division of labour whereby work is divided into small units, each of which is performed repetitively by an individual worker. Some motivational theories suggest that the boredom and alienation caused by the division of labour can actually cause efficiency to fall.

Chapter 12. Human resource management

Job rotation	Job rotation is an approach to management development where an individual is moved through a schedule of assignments designed to give him or her a breadth of exposure to the entire operation.
	Job rotation is also practiced to allow qualified employees to gain more insights into the processes of a company, and to reduce boredom and increase job satisfaction through job variation.
	The term Job rotation can also mean the scheduled exchange of persons in offices, especially in public offices, prior to the end of incumbency or the legislative period.
Autonomous work group	In business management, an Autonomous work group is a group encouraged to manage its own work and working practices. The concept of an Autonomous work group was developed by Eric Trist at the Tavistock Institute in London, England after the end of World War II. Involving the working team to decide for itself how the work should be carried out, and distributed among members.
Empowerment	Empowerment refers to increasing the spiritual, political, social, or economic strength of individuals and communities. It often involves the empowered developing confidence in their own capacities.
	The term Empowerment covers a vast landscape of meanings, interpretations, definitions and disciplines ranging from psychology and philosophy to the highly commercialized self-help industry and motivational sciences.
Job enrichment	Job enrichment is an attempt to motivate employees by giving them the opportunity to use the range of their abilities. It is an idea that was developed by the American psychologist Frederick Hertzberg in the 1950s. It can be contrasted to job enlargement which simply increases the number of tasks without changing the challenge.
Theory Z	Theory Z is a name applied to three distinctly different psychological theories. One was developed by Abraham H. Maslow in his paper Theory Z and the other is Dr. William Ouchi`s so-called `Japanese Management` style popularized during the Asian economic boom of the 1980s. The third was developed by W. J. Reddin in Managerial Effectiveness.

Chapter 12. Human resource management

Maslow's Theory Z' In contrast to Theory X, which stated that workers inherently dislike and avoid work and must be driven to it, and Theory Y, which stated that work is natural and can be a source of satisfaction when aimed at higher order human psychological needs.

For Ouchi, Theory Z focused on increasing employee loyalty to the company by providing a job for life with a strong focus on the well-being of the employee, both on and off the job. According to Ouchi, Theory Z management tends to promote stable employment, high productivity, and high employee morale and satisfaction.

Remuneration

Remuneration is pay or salary, typically a monetary payment for services rendered, as in an employment. Usage of the word is considered formal.

Performance related pay

Performance related pay is money paid to someone relating to how well he or she works at the workplace. Car salesmen, production line workers, for example, may be paid in this way, or through commission.

Business theorist Frederick Winslow Taylor was a great supporter of this method of payment, which is often referred to as Performance related pay. He believed money was the main incentive for increased productivity and introducing the widely used concept of `piece work`.

Chapter 13. New product development

Performance measurement	Performance measurement is the process whereby an organization establishes the parameters within which programs, investments, and acquisitions are reaching the desired results. This process of measuring performance often requires the use of statistical evidence to determine progress toward specific defined organizational objectives.
Time to market	In commerce, Time to market is the length of time it takes from a product being conceived until its being available for sale. Time to market is important in industries where products are outmoded quickly. A common assumption is that Time to market matters most for first-of-a-kind products, but actually the leader often has the luxury of time, while the clock is clearly running for the followers.
Product	When a Product reaches the maturity stage of the Product life cycle, a company may choose to operate strategies to extend the life of the Product. If the Product is predicted to continue to be successful or an upgrade is soon to be released the company can use various methods to keep sales, else the Product will be left as is to continue to the decline stage. Examples of extension strategies are: · Discounted price · Increased advertising · Accessing another market abroad
Idea generation	In business and engineering, new product development is the term used to describe the complete process of bringir g a new product or service to market. There are two parallel paths involved in the NPD process: one involves the Idea Generation, product design and detail engineering; the other involves market research and marketing analysis. Companies typically see new product development as the first stage in generating and commercializing new products within the overall strategic process of product life cycle management used to maintain or grow their market share.
Prototype	A Prototype is an original type, form, or instance of something serving as a typical example, basis, or standard for other things of the same category.

Chapter 13. New product development

Innovation	Innovation is a change in the thought process for doing something or `new stuff that is made useful`. It may refer to an incremental emergent or radical and revolutionary changes in thinking, products, processes, or organizations. Following Schumpeter (1934), contributors to the scholarly literature on Innovation typically distinguish between invention, an idea made manifest, and Innovation, ideas applied successfully in practice.
Disruptive innovation	Disruptive innovation is a term used in business and technology literature to describe innovations that improve a product or service in ways that the market does not expect, typically by lowering price or designing for a different set of consumers. In contrast to `Disruptive innovation`, a `sustaining` innovation does not have an effect on existing markets. Sustaining innovations may be either `discontinuous` (i.e. `transformational`) or `continuous` (i.e. `evolutionary`).
Product design	Product design is concerned with the efficient and effective generation and development of ideas through a process that leads to new products. Product designers conceptualize and evaluate ideas, making them tangible through products in a more systematic approach. Their role is to combine art, science and technology to create tangible three-dimensional goods.
Taguchi methods	Taguchi methods are statistical methods developed by Genichi Taguchi to improve the quality of manufactured goods, and more recently also applied to, engineering, biotechnology, marketing and advertising. Professional statisticians have welcomed the goals and improvements brought about by Taguchi methods, particularly by Taguchi`s development of designs for studying variation, but have criticized the inefficiency of some of Taguchi`s proposals.
Mass customization	Mass customization, in marketing, manufacturing, call centres and management, is the use of flexible computer-aided manufacturing systems to produce custom output. Those systems combine the low unit costs of mass production processes with the flexibility of individual customization. Mass customization is the new frontier in business competition for both manufacturing and service industries.

Chapter 14. Performance measurement

Performance measurement	Performance measurement is the process whereby an organization establishes the parameters within which programs, investments, and acquisitions are reaching the desired results.
	This process of measuring performance often requires the use of statistical evidence to determine progress toward specific defined organizational objectives.
Balanced scorecard	The Balanced scorecard is a strategic performance management tool for measuring whether the smaller-scale operational activities of a company are aligned with its larger-scale objectives in terms of vision and strategy.
	By focusing not only on financial outcomes but also on the operational, marketing and developmental inputs to these, the Balanced scorecard helps provide a more comprehensive view of a business, which in turn helps organizations act in their best long-term interests. This tool is also being used to address business response to climate change and greenhouse gas emissions.
Best practice	A Best practice is a technique, method, process, activity, incentive, or reward which conventional wisdom regards as more effective at delivering a particular outcome than any other technique, method, process, etc. when applied to a particular condition or circumstance. The idea is that with proper processes, checks, and testing, a desired outcome can be delivered with fewer problems and unforeseen complications.
Targets	Targets is a thriller film written, produced and directed by Peter Bogdanovich.
	The story concerns an insurance agent and Vietnam veteran, played by Tim O`Kelly, who murders his wife and mother and then goes on a shooting rampage from atop a Los Angeles oil refinery. When police start to close in on him, he flees to and resumes his shootings at a drive-in theater where an aging horror film actor is making a final promotional appearance.
Benchmarking	Benchmarking is the process of comparing one`s business processes and performance metrics to industry bests and/or best practices from other industries. Dimensions typically measured are quality, time, and cost. Improvements from learning mean doing things better, faster, and cheaper.

Chapter 14. Performance measurement

Performance improvement	Performance improvement is the concept of measuring the output of a particular process or procedure, then modifying the process or procedure to increase the output, increase efficiency, or increase the effectiveness of the process or procedure. The concept of Performance improvement can be applied to either individual performance such as an athlete or organisational performance such as a racing team or a commercial enterprise. In Organisational development, Performance improvement is the concept of organizational change in which the managers and governing body of an organisation put into place and manage a programme which measures the current level of performance of the organization and then generates ideas for modifying organisational behavior and infrastructure which are put into place to achieve higher output.
Business process	A Business process or business method is a collection of related, structured activities or tasks that produce a specific service or product for a particular customer or customers. It often can be visualized with a flowchart as a sequence of activities. There are three types of Business processes: · Management processes, the processes that govern the operation of a system. Typical management processes include `Corporate Governance` and `Strategic Management`. · Operational processes, processes that constitute the core business and create the primary value stream. Typical operational processes are Purchasing, Manufacturing, Marketing and Sales. · Supporting processes, which support the core processes. Examples include Accounting, Recruitment, Technical support.
Business process reengineering	Business process reengineering is, in computer science and management, an approach aiming at improvements by means of elevating efficiency and effectiveness of the business process that exist within and across organizations. The key to Business process reengineering is for organizations to look at their business processes from a `clean slate` perspective and determine how they can best construct these processes to improve how they conduct business. Business process reengineering Cycle. Business process reengineering is also known as Business process reengineering, Business Process Redesign, Business Transformation, or Business Process Change Management.

Chapter 14. Performance measurement

Continuous

In probability theory, a probability distribution is called continuous if its cumulative distribution function is continuous . This is equivalent to saying that for random variables X with the distribution in question, Pr[X = a] = 0 for all real numbers a, i.e.: the probability that X attains the value a is zero, for any number a. If the distribution of X is continuous then X is called a continuous random variable.

Chapter 15. Current trends and emerging issues

Factory	A Factory is an industrial building where laborers manufacture goods or supervise machines processing one product into another. Most modern factories have large warehouses or warehouse-like facilities that contain heavy equipment used for assembly line production. Typically, factories gather and concentrate resources: laborers, capital and plant.
Supply network	A Supply network is a pattern of temporal and spatial processes carried out at facility nodes and over distribution links, which adds value for customers through the manufacturing and delivery of products. It comprises the general state of business affairs in which all kinds of material are transformed and moved between various value-add points to maximize the value added for customers. A supply chain is a special instance of a Supply network in which raw materials, intermediate materials and finished goods are procured exclusively as products through a chain of processes that supply one another.
Information and communication technologies	Information and communication technologies is an umbrella term that covers all technical means for processing and communicating information. While this technically encompasses pre-digital technologies, including paper-based writing, it is most often used to describe digital technologies including methods for communication (communication protocols, transmission techniques, communications equipment, media (communication)), as well as techniques for storing and processing information (computing, data storage, etc). The term has gained popularity partially due to the convergence of information technology (IT) and telecom technology.
Cost	In business, retail, and accounting, a Cost is the value of money that has been used up to produce something, and hence is not available for use anymore. In economics, a Cost is an alternative that is given up as a result of a decision. In business, the Cost may be one of acquisition, in which case the amount of money expended to acquire it is counted as Cost.
Discontinuity	Continuous functions are of utmost importance in mathematics and applications. However, not all functions are continuous. If a function is not continuous at a point in its domain, one says that it has a discontinuity there.
Business continuity	Business continuity is the activity performed by an organization to ensure that critical business functions will be available to customers, suppliers, regulators, and other entities that must have access to those functions. These activities include many daily chores such as project management, system backups, change control, and help desk. Business continuity is not something implemented at the time of a disaster; Business continuity refers to those activities performed daily to maintain service, consistency, and recoverability.

Chapter 15. Current trends and emerging issues

Business continuity planning	Business continuity planning OR Business continuity ' Resilency planning (BCRP) is the creation and validation of a practiced logistical plan for how an organization will recover and restore partially or completely interrupted critical (urgent) functions within a predetermined time after a disaster or extended disruption. The logistical plan is called a business continuity plan. The intended effect of Business continuity planning is to ensure Business continuity, which is an ongoing state or methodology governing how business is conducted.
Environmentalism	Environmentalism is a broad philosophy and social movement regarding concerns for environmental conservation and improvement of the state of the environment. Environmentalism and environmental concerns are often represented with the color green. Environmentalism can also be defined as a social movement that seeks to influence the political process by lobbying, activism, and education in order to protect natural resources and ecosystems.
Social responsibility	Social responsibility is an ethical or ideological theory that business should not function amorally but instead should contribute to the welfare of their communities and an entity whether it is a government, corporation, organization or individual has a big responsibility to society at large. This responsibility can be `negative`, meaning there is exemption from blame or liability, or it can be `positive,` meaning there is a responsibility to act beneficently (proactive stance).
Knowledge management	Knowledge management comprises a range of strategies and practices used in an organization to identify, create, represent, distribute, and enable adoption of insights and experiences. Such insights and experiences comprise knowledge, either embodied in individuals or embedded in organizational processes or practice.
Activity-based costing	Activity-based costing is a costing model that identifies activities in an organization and assigns the cost of each activity resource to all products and services according to the actual consumption by each: it assigns more indirect costs (overhead) into direct costs. In this way an organization can precisely estimate the cost of its individual products and services for the purposes of identifying and eliminating those which are unprofitable and lowering the prices of those which are overpriced. In a business organization, the Activity based costing methodology assigns an organization`s resource costs through activities to the products and services provided to its customers.

Chapter 15. Current trends and emerging issues

ABC analysis	ABC analysis is a business term used to define an inventory categorization technique often used in materials management. It is also known as Selective Inventory Control. ABC analysis provides a mechanism for identifying items that will have a significant impact on overall inventory cost, whilst also providing a mechanism for identifying different categories of stock that will require different management and controls.
Construction aggregate	Construction aggregate is a broad category of coarse particulate material used in construction, including sand, gravel, crushed stone, slag, recycled concrete and geosynthetic aggregates. Aggregates are a component of composite materials such as concrete and asphalt concrete; the aggregate serves as reinforcement to add strength to the overall composite material. Due to the relatively high hydraulic conductivity value as compared to most soils, aggregates are widely used in drainage applications such as foundation and french drains, septic drain fields, retaining wall drains, and road side edge drains.
Automation	Automation is the use of control systems and information technologies reducing the need for human intervention. In the scope of industrialization, Automation is a step beyond mechanization. Whereas mechanization provided human operators with machinery to assist them with the muscular requirements of work, Automation greatly reduces the need for human sensory and mental requirements as well.
Back office	A Back office is a part of most corporations where tasks dedicated to running the company itself take place. The term comes from the building layout of early companies where the front office would contain the sales and other customer-facing staff and the Back office would be those manufacturing or developing the products or involved in administration but without being seen by customers. Although the operations of a Back office are usually not given a lot of consideration, they are a major contributor to a business.
Balanced scorecard	The Balanced scorecard is a strategic performance management tool for measuring whether the smaller-scale operational activities of a company are aligned with its larger-scale objectives in terms of vision and strategy. By focusing not only on financial outcomes but also on the operational, marketing and developmental inputs to these, the Balanced scorecard helps provide a more comprehensive view of a business, which in turn helps organizations act in their best long-term interests. This tool is also being used to address business response to climate change and greenhouse gas emissions.

Chapter 15. Current trends and emerging issues

Competence	Competence is the ability to perform a specific task, action or function successfully. Competence, in human resource is a standardized requirement for an individual to properly perform a specific job
Cross-functional team	A cross-functional team is a group of employees from various functional areas of the organization - research, engineering, marketing, finance, human resources, and operations, for example - who are all focused on a specific objective and are responsible to work as a team to improve coordination and innovation across divisions and resolve mutual problems.
Disintermediation	In economics, Disintermediation is the removal of intermediaries in a supply chain: `cutting out the middleman`. Instead of going through traditional distribution channels, which had some type of intermediate (such as a distributor, wholesaler, broker, or agent), companies may now deal with every customer directly, for example via the Internet. One important factor is a drop in the cost of servicing customers directly.
Disruptive innovation	Disruptive innovation is a term used in business and technology literature to describe innovations that improve a product or service in ways that the market does not expect, typically by lowering price or designing for a different set of consumers.
	In contrast to `Disruptive innovation`, a `sustaining` innovation does not have an effect on existing markets. Sustaining innovations may be either `discontinuous` (i.e. `transformational`) or `continuous` (i.e. `evolutionary`).
Division of labour	Division of labour is the specialization of cooperative labour in specific, circumscribed tasks and roles. Historically an increasingly complex division of labor is closely associated with the growth of total output and trade, the rise of capitalism, and of the complexity of industrialization processes. Division of labor was also a method used by the neolithics and paleolithics to categorize different jobs, and divide them to skilled members of a society.
Electronic business	Electronic business may be defined as the utilization of information and communication technologies (ICT) in support of all the activities of business. Commerce constitutes the exchange of products and services between businesses, groups and individuals and can be seen as one of the essential activities of any business. Electronic commerce focuses on the use of ICT to enable the external activities and relationships of the business with individuals, groups and other businesses.

Chapter 15. Current trends and emerging issues

Chapter 15. Current trends and emerging issues

E-commerce	E-commerce consists of the buying and selling of products or services over electronic systems such as the Internet and other computer networks. The amount of trade conducted electronically has grown extraordinarily with widespread Internet usage. The use of commerce is conducted in this way, spurring and drawing on innovations in electronic funds transfer, supply chain management, Internet marketing, online transaction processing, electronic data interchange (EDI), inventory management systems, and automated data collection systems.
Performance measurement	Performance measurement is the process whereby an organization establishes the parameters within which programs, investments, and acquisitions are reaching the desired results.
	This process of measuring performance often requires the use of statistical evidence to determine progress toward specific defined organizational objectives.
GNI per capita	GNI per capita is the dollar value of a country`s final income in a year (Gross National Income), divided by its population. It reflects the average income of a country`s citizens. Knowing a country`s GNI per capita is a good first step toward understanding the country`s economic strengths and needs, as well as the general standard of living enjoyed by the average citizen. A country`s GNI per capita tends to be closely linked with other indicators that measure the social, economic, and environmental well-being of the country and its people.
E-learning	E-learning comprises all forms of electronically supported learning and teaching, which are procedural in character and aim to effect the construction of knowledge with reference to individual experience, practice and knowledge of the learner. Information and communication systems, whether networked or not, serve as specific media to implement the learning process.
	E-learning is essentially the computer and network enabled transfer of skills and knowledge.
Economies of scale	Economies of scale, in microeconomics, refers to the cost advantages that a business obtains due to expansion. There are factors that cause a producer`s average cost per unit to fall as the scale of output is increased. `Economies of scale` is a long run concept and refers to reductions in unit cost as the size of a facility and the usage levels of other inputs increase.

Chapter 15. Current trends and emerging issues

Economies of scope	Economies of scope are conceptually similar to economies of scale. Whereas economies of scale primarily refer to efficiencies associated with supply-side changes, such as increasing or decreasing the scale of production, of a single product type, Economies of scope refer to efficiencies primarily associated with demand-side changes, such as increasing or decreasing the scope of marketing and distribution, of different types of products. Economies of scope are one of the main reasons for such marketing strategies as product bundling, product lining, and family branding.
Empowerment	Empowerment refers to increasing the spiritual, political, social, or economic strength of individuals and communities. It often involves the empowered developing confidence in their own capacities.
	The term Empowerment covers a vast landscape of meanings, interpretations, definitions and disciplines ranging from psychology and philosophy to the highly commercialized self-help industry and motivational sciences.
Forecasting	Forecasting is the process of estimation in unknown situations. Prediction is a similar, but more general term. Both can refer to estimation of time series, cross-sectional or longitudinal data.
Front office	Front office is a business term that refers to a company's departments that come in contact with clients, including the marketing, sales, and service departments.
	The Front office welcomes guests to the accommodation section: meeting and greeting them, taking and organizing reservations, allocating check in and out of rooms, organizing porter service, issuing keys and other security arrangements, passing on messages to customers and settling the accounts.
Globalization	Globalization describes a process by which regional economies, societies, and cultures have become integrated through a global network of communication, transportation, and trade. The term is sometimes used to refer specifically to economic Globalization: the integration of national economies into the international economy through trade, foreign direct investment, capital flows, migration, and the spread of technology. However, Globalization is usually recognized as being driven by a combination of economic, technological, sociocultural, political, and biological factors.

99

Chapter 15. Current trends and emerging issues

Groupthink	Groupthink is a type of thought within a deeply cohesive in-group whose members try to minimize conflict and reach consensus without critically testing, analyzing, and evaluating ideas. It is a second potential negative consequence of group cohesion.

Irving Janis studied a number of American Foreign policy `disasters` such as failure to anticipate the Japanese attack on Pearl Harbor ; the Bay of Pigs fiasco (1961) when the US adminstration sought to overthrow Cuban Government of Fidel Castro; and the prosecution of the Vietnam War (1964-67) by President Lyndon Johnson. |
Human resources	Human resources is a term used to describe the individuals who comprise the workforce of an organization, although it is also applied in labor economics to, for example, business sectors or even whole nations. Human resources is also the name of the function within an organization charged with the overall responsibility for implementing strategies and policies relating to the management of individuals (i.e. the Human resources).
Internationalization	In economics, Internationalization has been viewed as a process of increasing involvement of enterprises in international markets, although there is no agreed definition of Internationalization or international entrepreneurship. There are several Internationalization theories which try to explain why there are international activities.
Job description	A Job description is a list of the general tasks, or functions, and responsibilities of a position. Typically, it also includes to whom the position reports, specifications such as the qualifications needed by the person in the job, salary range for the position, etc. A Job description is usually developed by conducting a job analysis, which includes examining the tasks and sequences of tasks necessary to perform the job.
Lean manufacturing	Lean manufacturing is a production practice that considers the expenditure of resources for any goal other than the creation of value for the end customer to be wasteful, and thus a target for elimination. Working from the perspective of the customer who consumes a product or service, `value` is defined as any action or process that a customer would be willing to pay for. Basically, lean is centered on preserving value with less work.
Market access	Market access for goods in the WTO means the conditions, tariff and non-tariff measures, agreed by members for the entry of specific goods into their markets. Tariff commitments for goods are set out in each member's schedules of concessions on goods. The schedules represent commitments not to apply tariffs above the listed rates -- these rates are `bound`.

Chapter 15. Current trends and emerging issues

Mass customization	Mass customization, in marketing, manufacturing, call centres and management, is the use of flexible computer-aided manufacturing systems to produce custom output. Those systems combine the low unit costs of mass production processes with the flexibility of individual customization.
	Mass customization is the new frontier in business competition for both manufacturing and service industries.
Resource	A Resource is any physical or virtual entity of limited availability that needs to be consumed to obtain a benefit from it. In most cases, commercial or even ethic factors require Resource allocation through Resource management.
G-code	G-code are functions in the Numerical control programming language. The G-codes are the codes that position the tool and do the actual work, as opposed to M-codes, that manages the machine, T for tool-related codes. S and F are tool-Speed and tool-Feed, and finally D-codes for tool compensation.
Operations management	Operations management is an area of business concerned with the production of goods and services, and involves the responsibility of ensuring that business operations are efficient in terms of using as little resource as needed, and effective in terms of meeting customer requirements. It is concerned with managing the process that converts inputs (in the forms of materials, labor and energy) into outputs (in the form of goods and services).
	Operations traditionally refers to the production of goods and services separately, although the distinction between these two main types of operations is increasingly difficult to make as manufacturers tend to merge product and service offerings.
Outsourcing	Outsourcing often refers to the process of contracting to a third-party. While Outsourcing may be viewed as a component to the growing division of labor encompassing all societies, the term did not enter the English-speaking lexicon until the 1980s. Since the 1980s, transnational corporations have increased subcontracting across national boundaries.
Person specification	The Person specification is an extension of the job description. It is a profile of the type of person needed to do a job and is produced along with a job description following a job analysis.

Chapter 15. Current trends and emerging issues

Quality assurance	Quality assurance refers to a program for the systematic monitoring and evaluation of the various aspects of a project, service, or facility to ensure that standards of quality are being met. It is important to realize also that quality is determined by the program sponsor. Quality assurance cannot absolutely guarantee the production of quality products, unfortunately, but makes this more likely.
Quality circle	A Quality circle is a volunteer group composed of workers (or even students), usually under the leadership of their supervisor (but they can elect a team leader), who are trained to identify, analyse and solve work-related problems and present their solutions to management in order to improve the performance of the organization, and motivate and enrich the work of employees. When matured, true Quality circles become self-managing, having gained the confidence of management.
Quality control	Quality control is a process by which entities review the quality of all factors involved in production. This approach places an emphasis on three aspects: · Elements such as controls, job management, defined and well managed processes, performance and integrity criteria, and identification of records · Competence, such as knowledge, skills, experience, and qualifications · Soft elements, such as personnel integrity, confidence, organizational culture, motivation, team spirit, and quality relationships. The quality of the outputs is at risk if any of these three aspects is deficient in any way. Quality control emphasizes testing of products to uncover defects, and reporting to management who make the decision to allow or deny the release, whereas quality assurance attempts to improve and stabilize production, and associated processes, to avoid, or at least minimize, issues that led to the defects in the first place.
Quality function deployment	Quality function deployment is a `method to transform user demands into design quality, to deploy the functions forming quality, and to deploy methods for achieving the design quality into subsystems and component parts, and ultimately to specific elements of the manufacturing process.` , as described by Dr. Yoji Akao, who originally developed Quality function deployment in Japan in 1966, when the author combined his work in quality assurance and quality control points with function deployment used in Value Engineering.

Chapter 15. Current trends and emerging issues

Quality function deployment is designed to help planners focus on characteristics of a new or existing product or service from the viewpoints of market segments, company, or technology-development needs. The technique yields graphs and matrices.

Scientific management	Scientific management is a theory of management that analyzes and synthesizes workflows, with the objective of improving labor productivity. The core ideas of the theory were developed by Frederick Winslow Taylor in the 1880s and 1890s, and were first published in his monographs, Shop Management (1905) and The Principles of Scientific management. He began trying to discover a way for workers to increase their efficiency when he was the foreperson at the Midvale Steele Company in 1875. Taylor believed that decisions based upon tradition and rules of thumb should be replaced by precise procedures developed after careful study of an individual at work.
Theory Z	Theory Z is a name applied to three distinctly different psychological theories. One was developed by Abraham H. Maslow in his paper Theory Z and the other is Dr. William Ouchi`s so-called `Japanese Management` style popularized during the Asian economic boom of the 1980s. The third was developed by W. J. Reddin in Managerial Effectiveness. Maslow`s Theory Z` In contrast to Theory X, which stated that workers inherently dislike and avoid work and must be driven to it, and Theory Y, which stated that work is natural and can be a source of satisfaction when aimed at higher order human psychological needs.
	For Ouchi, Theory Z focused on increasing employee loyalty to the company by providing a job for life with a strong focus on the well-being of the employee, both on and off the job. According to Ouchi, Theory Z management tends to promote stable employment, high productivity, and high employee morale and satisfaction.
Product	When a Product reaches the maturity stage of the Product life cycle, a company may choose to operate strategies to extend the life of the Product. If the Product is predicted to continue to be successful or an upgrade is soon to be released the company can use various methods to keep sales, else the Product will be left as is to continue to the decline stage.
	Examples of extension strategies are:
	· Discounted price
	· Increased advertising

· Accessing another market abroad

Supply chain

A Supply chain is a system of organizations, people, technology, activities, information and resources involved in moving a product or service from supplier to customer. Supply chain activities transform natural resources, raw materials and components into a finished product that is delivered to the end customer. In sophisticated Supply chain systems, used products may re-enter the Supply chain at any point where residual value is recyclable.

Time to market

In commerce, Time to market is the length of time it takes from a product being conceived until its being available for sale. Time to market is important in industries where products are outmoded quickly. A common assumption is that Time to market matters most for first-of-a-kind products, but actually the leader often has the luxury of time, while the clock is clearly running for the followers.

Trade-off

A Trade-off is a situation that involves losing one quality or aspect of something in return for gaining another quality or aspect. It implies a decision to be made with full comprehension of both the upside and downside of a particular choice.

In economics the term is expressed as opportunity cost, referring to the most preferred alternative given up.

Vertical integration

In microeconomics and management, the term Vertical integration describes a style of management control. Vertically integrated companies in a supply chain are united through a common owner. Usually each member of the supply chain produces a different product or (market-specific) service, and the products combine to satisfy a common need.

Yield management

Yield management is the process of understanding, anticipating and influencing consumer behavior in order to maximize revenue or profits from a fixed, perishable resource (such as airline seats or hotel room reservations).

The challenge is to sell the right resources to the right customer at the right time for the right price. This process can result in price discrimination, where a firm charges customers consuming otherwise identical goods or services a different price for doing so.

Lightning Source UK Ltd.
Milton Keynes UK
UKOW02f0022231013

219580UK00003B/157/P